WELCOME TO GOD'S FAMILY

Grace Pathway Milestone 1

BILL GIOVANNETTI

Endurant Press

© Copyright Bill Giovannetti 2018. All Rights Reserved.

No part of this book may be reproduced or transmitted in any form or by any means, digital, electronic or mechanical, including photocopying, recording, or by an information storage and retrieval system—except by a reviewer who may quote brief passages in a review to be printed in a magazine, newspaper, or on the Web—without permission in writing from the publisher.

Although the author and publisher have made every effort to ensure the accuracy and completeness of information contained in this book, the same assumes no responsibility for errors, inaccuracies, omissions, or any inconsistency herein. Any slights of people, places, or organizations are unintentional. All persons and situations mentioned in this book are fictionalized. Any resemblance to any person, living or dead, is strictly coincidental. Nothing herein shall be construed as a substitute for personal, pastoral, or professional counseling or therapy.

ISBN E-book edition: 978-1-946654-09-0

ISBN Print edition: 978-1-946654-08-3

All scripture quotations, unless otherwise indicated, are taken from the *New King James Version* (R). Copyright © 1982 by Thomas Nelson, Inc. Used by permission. All rights reserved.

Scripture quotations marked (NLT) are taken from the *Holy Bible, New Living Translation,* copyright © 1996, 2004, 2007 by Tyndale House Foundation. Used by permission of Tyndale House Publishers, Inc., Carol Stream, Illinois 60188. All rights reserved.

For additional resources, please visit maxgrace.com.

 Created with Vellum

WHAT'S IN THIS BOOK?

Welcome to God's Family!

That's what I say to each person at my church who responds to an invitation to receive Jesus as their Savior. What an awesome moment! Some of these friends are smiling the biggest smile I've ever seen. Others have a tear or two rolling down their face. There are some who seem pretty unemotional. Others are hard to read. The emotional range is huge.

But all of them find themselves in that incredible moment of crossing a cosmic threshold from spiritual death to spiritual life with God forever.

This little book is for you — for every person who has said "Yes" to the Savior, Jesus.

In this booklet, we'll go over what it means to be saved. I want to help you understand what a big thing salvation is, and to know exactly how it happened.

You are beginning a journey, and this booklet — along with each one that follows, will be your travel guide. This will be the best trip of your life! It will be amazing, and wonderful, intimidating, and liberating all at once.

I'm super-excited to see what God does in your life. Keep moving forward. Don't let setbacks turn into exit ramps. Keep moving forward, and see the awesomeness that God has woven into your truest, deepest self.

Welcome to God's Family.

And welcome to the first milestone along the Grace Pathway. God Saves You. Now, let's figure out what that means.

WE ARE ALL THE SAME

You may have been given this booklet because you just received Jesus. That's awesome. If you could see God right now, you would see a huge smile on his face. When a person becomes part of God's family, the Bible says God throws a gigantic party in heaven, and even the angels join the celebration. Yes, God is that happy whenever a person crosses the line into salvation.

It doesn't matter what kind of person you have been. You might be very successful. You may be financially secure. You might have an excellent family. You might look good, smell good, and be good. Even so, the very best thing about you now is that you have Jesus as your Savior.

On the other hand, you might come from a rough background. You might even be an addict, a criminal, or a very broken person. It could be you barely scrape by. Or your life is a wreck. Maybe you wish to God you could erase the choices of your past. Or you're desperate. Angry. Afraid. You might feel your dark side owns you. Even so, God has scrubbed your past, guaranteed your future, and entered your present, now that you have Jesus as your Savior.

No matter how low you've sunk or how high you have risen, we all need Jesus, and we are all equal at his feet. This is the beauty of salvation.

"Salvation" is one of those religious words that confuses people. So let's end the confusion right now. What is salvation and why is it so important?

WHAT IS SALVATION?

— SALVATION IS THE WONDERFUL ACT OF GOD IN DELIVERING A PERSON FROM ALL THE DESTRUCTIVE FORCES IN THEIR LIFE, AND SETTING THEM IN A PLACE OF GOODNESS AND BLESSING IN THIS LIFE AND FOREVER.

When you think of the word "salvation," it basically means to rescue. God's salvation is a rescue operation. When God saves you, he rescues you and he sets you in a place of wholeness and safety forever.

What does he rescue you from? He rescues you from the dark, nasty force in your life that breaks your heart and makes you hurt other people. That force is called SIN. If you don't like that word, call it something else. The main thing God saves you from is sin and all its gnarly outgrowths in your life.

Nobody can do this but God. Nobody can forgive sin, but God alone. Nobody else can yank out sin by the roots and make you qualified for heaven.

Salvation is a beautiful gift from God. It is a miracle. You can picture salvation as a gift-package. It is one very big gift with a lot of smaller gifts inside. Each one is a wonder to unwrap and enjoy.

Salvation is the biggest thing that has ever happened to you. Of all the big deals in your life, salvation is the biggest deal of all. That's why Christians get so excited when they hear about somebody getting saved.

The only reason salvation even exists is because of Jesus. The sacrifice he made when he died and rose again makes salvation possible. Without him, there could be no salvation for anybody.

I was saved as a little boy — an adorable, cute, fidgety seven-ish-year old boy — in Chicago. The details are fuzzy, but I heard about Jesus in a tiny church, and God saved me when I was young.

You may have been saved as a kid too. Or, you might have been saved as an adult. Or as a senior citizen. It makes no difference. The story of *when* you crossed the line into God's family has different details on the outside, but on the inside it's the same for all of us, young and old alike. When it comes to our need for salvation, we're all the same.

If life with God is a mansion, then the gospel is the threshold, and being saved is the moment you step through the door. For all of eternity you get to enjoy, explore, and share life in the mansion of God's wonderful salvation!

Here are some of my favorite verses about salvation:

- For God so loved the world that He gave His only begotten Son, that whoever believes in Him should not perish but have everlasting life. (John 3:16)
- He has delivered us from the power of darkness and conveyed *us* into the kingdom of the Son of His love. (Colossians 1:13)
- God saved you by his special favor when you believed. And you can't take credit for this; it is a gift from God. Salvation is not a reward for the good things we have done, so none of us can boast about it. (Ephesians 2:8, 9, NLT)

And here are my top five benefits of being saved:

1. HEAVEN. The only way to go to heaven when we die is by being saved before we die. *"And this is what God has testified: He has given us eternal life, and this life is in his Son. So whoever has God's Son has life; whoever does not have his Son does not have life" (1 John 5:11, 12, NLT)*.
2. FORGIVENESS. When God saves you, he erases your guilt and shame forever. He did this when Jesus died, by punishing Christ for your sins instead of punishing you. He was your substitute. He took your place. This is so incredibly important! God forgives you not

because you become a wonderful person. The power of forgiveness is not in you. The power of forgiveness is all wrapped up in the sacrificial death of Jesus on the Cross. *"The next day John saw Jesus coming toward him, and said, 'Behold! The Lamb of God who takes away the sin of the world!'" (John 1:29).*

3. PRESENCE. From the very first nano-second of your salvation, and forever to the ages of eternity, you have God's own personal presence. He is with you. He is in you. You are never alone, because you have the presence of God with you. *"For He Himself has said, 'I will never leave you nor forsake you.' So we may boldly say: 'The Lord is my helper; I will not fear. What can man do to me?'" (Hebrews 13:5).*

4. PEACE. To have salvation is to have peace with God. You don't have to fear him or avoid him. Salvation ended your conflict with God and brought you into harmony with him forever. *"Therefore, since we have been made right in God's sight by faith, we have peace with God because of what Jesus Christ our Lord has done for us" (Romans 5:1, NLT).*

5. A FRESH START. Salvation makes you a totally new person with a brand new start. Every day is a new day with God, and you don't have to be stuck with a messed up past anymore. *"Therefore, if anyone is in Christ, he is a new creation; old things have passed away; behold, all things have become new." (2 Corinthians 5:17)*

There are plenty more benefits, but this is a pretty incredible start!

Now, let's go deeper and break it down. Exactly how does God give salvation, and what do we have to do to receive it?

WHAT IS THE GOSPEL?

Salvation is the gift you receive. The Gospel explains God's directions on how you receive it. So, what is the Gospel?

> — THE GOSPEL IS THE GOOD NEWS OF ALL THAT GOD HAS DONE FOR US IN JESUS, BECAUSE OF HIS DEATH ON THE CROSS AND HIS RESURRECTION FROM THE DEAD.

1. ITS DEFINITION

The gospel is the entry way into the family and plan of God. If life with God is a mansion, the gospel is the doorway into the mansion. Unless you have crossed the threshold of the gospel, you are still outside.

Think of it this way. In the Bible, there are thousands of amazing truths. Tens of thousands. Promises. Teachings. Commands. Ideas. Stories.

There's a whole lot of stuff in this great big Bible.

The gospel is a subset of all those truths. The gospel is a group of specific teachings in the Bible. So here is our definition of the gospel.

The gospel is the irreducible minimum of truths a person must hear and respond to in order to be saved. Those truths focus on Jesus — his death on the cross and his resurrection from the grave — as our only hope of salvation and life with God.

> How then shall they call on Him in whom they have not believed? And how shall they believe in Him of whom they have not heard? And how shall they hear without a preacher? (Romans 10:14)

This verse points to a kind of spiritual chain-reaction. If we take it backwards you have somebody communicating the gospel, which leads to somebody hearing the gospel, which leads to someone believing the gospel and calling on God for salvation. That's the pattern.

2. ITS NATURE

By nature, the gospel is good news. That's what the word Gospel means in Old English. Good news.

That means that when a person first hears the gospel, it feels too good to be true.

Have you ever felt that way about what Jesus offers you?

It's good news because it offers a free gift.

It's good news because it wipes human sweat off the table.

It's good news because it's a gift.

It's good news because it is free.

It's good news because it is paid for by Christ.

It's good news because it is finished.

It's good news because it is once for all.

It's good news because it never goes away.

It's good news because it only requires that you be a sinner and know it.

It's good news because you don't earn it.

It's good news because you don't deserve it.

It's good news because it requires zero performance, zero improvement, zero obligation, zero duty, zero religious activity, and zero worthiness.

All of that is very good news, wouldn't you say?

It's good news because the gospel is soaked through with an awesome quality called GRACE.

Grace is God doing for you what you can't do for yourself, free of charge, based not on what you deserve, but on the blood of Calvary's Cross.

Grace is unmerited favor.

Grace is you, not earning, not deserving, not performing, not winning.

Grace is God paying all the price, and God breaking all the sweat.

The gospel is grace through and through. God never piles a burden on your back. He takes all the burden himself.

Truly, really, forever good news.

So the gospel defined is... "The gospel is the irreducible minimum of truths a person must hear and respond to in order to be saved."

And the nature of this subset of truth is that it is always and forever good news.

But we still haven't specified those truths; let's do that

now. Here is indispensable fact number 3 about the gospel:

3. ITS CORE

At the core of the gospel stands the Savior, crucified and risen again.

The core of the gospel is Jesus Christ, crucified and risen again. Here is the main Scripture to support this:

> For I delivered to you first of all that which I also received: that Christ died for our sins according to the Scriptures, and that He was buried, and that He rose again the third day according to the Scriptures. (1 Corinthians 15:3, 4)

Let's take those five little words: Christ died for our sins.

Five monosyllables. Any child can pronounce them.

Christ died... that part is *history*. If you had been there, you would have seen it.

For our sins... that part is *theology*. That part you need to have explained to you, taught to you, illuminated to you. That's what this little booklet is for.

What it means is that whatever had to happen to pay for your sins happened the day Christ died.

When he died, your sins were punished and judged and erased and paid for and condemned, not in you, but in Jesus.

Because he was condemned, there is no condemnation for you.

Because he died, you don't have to.

That is the indispensable core. That is the irreducible minimum.

The Cross was earth's darkest night, and grace's brightest dawn.

So let's review…

Definition: the gospel is the entryway into the family and plan of God.

Nature: the gospel is good news, the best news ever given to the world of humankind.

Core: the core of the gospel is Jesus Christ, crucified for your sins, and risen for your life.

Now, here's indispensable fact number 4:

4. ITS RESPONSE

The response to the gospel is simple faith. Just naked, simple faith plus nothing else. The gospel summons all people everywhere to simply believe on the Lord Jesus Christ.

> In Him you also trusted, after you heard the word of truth, the gospel of your salvation; in whom also, having believed, you were sealed with the Holy Spirit of promise." (Ephesians 1:13)

You trusted. You believed. These are the same thing. Synonyms. You trusted. You believed.

What does that mean?

It means you rested the weight of your hopes on Christ. You've placed your hope in Christ. You have believed in Jesus, and identified him as your *only hope* of salvation. Jesus, by his death and resurrection, is…

Your only hope to be forgiven.

Your only hope to be set free.

Your only hope to be adopted into God's forever family.

Your only hope to be welcomed into heaven some day.

Salvation comes by faith alone in Christ alone.

You trusted, you believed, you put your faith in Christ. And in that moment, you were sealed into the family of God.

That's what God has said so clearly in the Bible.

You trusted, you believed, you put your faith alone in Christ alone. And in that moment, you stepped out of the howling storms of religion and shame and sin and dysfunction and guilt... you stepped across the threshold into the warmth of eternal life, and the Holy Spirit slammed the door behind you. You are sealed into your salvation by the Holy Spirit of promise.

Faith.

Not works.

Not rituals.

Not moral improvement.

Not paying a price.

Not sacrifice, dedication, consecration, surrender or anything you do for God, give to God, or perform for God at all.

Faith means believing in what Jesus did for you rather than in what you do for God.

Anyone can have faith. Anyone can believe. Everyone has faith in something. It's the simplest thing in the world. Even a child can believe.

The human problem is not a lack of faith.

The human problem is that most people have not put their faith in Christ. They're believing in the wrong things — good works, religion, baptism, morality, or luck.

You need to believe the Gospel (Mark 1:15). In Christ.

One day you're going to die.

Aren't you glad you're reading this?

One day you're going to die. There you will stand, before the high court of heaven. God the judge will speak. "Give me one good reason," he will say. "Point to one good reason why I should let you into heaven."

Where will you point? To your own good deeds? Your good works? Your religion? Your obedience? Your morality? Your sparkling personality and stellar good looks? Where will you point?

I know where I'm pointing: I will point to Jesus Christ, and I will say, *He's all my reason and my only reason, and if Jesus is not enough, I've got no Plan B.*

Faith means pointing to Christ. It is putting all your hopes in him. It is un-pointing to everything else, and trusting exclusively in the Savior of your soul. Faith is an "unwork." It is stopping your labors and arduous efforts that you might rest in the work of Christ on Calvary's cross.

When your faith touches God's grace, the magic happens.

Have you ever put your faith in Christ as your Savior? You can do that right now.

How?

Well, how do you respond to an offer of a gift? You receive it.

Faith is receiving Christ and the eternal life he brings.

It is that simple.

You say yes, and you are born again.

Having believed, you were sealed... the Bible says. So

simple. How sad we make this more complicated than it needs to be!

The response to the gospel is faith alone in Christ alone.

Now, let's expand on that a bit.

WHAT MUST I DO?

The Bible makes it really simple for us. There is a beautiful story in the Bible where a jail guard is in trouble. God has just done a miracle, and broken the jail doors in order to set some of his people free. The jail guard is panicking. He falls on his knees and asks God's people, men named Paul and Silas, the all-important question.

He asks, "What must I do to be saved?"

At this point, the little religious tyrant in our hearts might come up with a whole list of duties: quit your job as a jail-thug, be a better person, go do a religious duty, perform good deeds, sacrifice something, and on and on. We are hopelessly addicted to the idea that God wants us to jump through hoops before he will accept us.

God's grace, and God's gospel should smash that idea into powdery nothingness.

When that jail guard asked what he had to do to be saved, here is the answer he received:

So they said, "Believe on the Lord Jesus Christ, and you will be saved, you and your household." (Acts 16:31)

Believe.
Believe on Jesus.

It's so ridiculously easy. It's as easy as receiving a free gift from someone who loves you.

Maybe you're ready right now to do that! That's tremendous! Here is a simple prayer you can pray to tell God that you are believing in Jesus.

One nice bonus note first: did you see the last three words of that Bible verse, "and your household"? That's an awesome promise that when *you* are saved, you will begin to influence your whole network of family and friends with the good news of the gospel. They might very well get saved too, as they hear about Jesus from you, and see the difference he makes in your life.

Okay. Here is a prayer you can say to God to express that you are believing in Jesus. It follows an ABC pattern.

Here's the prayer. If you are willing, you can pray this to God right now. Out loud or silently, it makes no difference.

---

1. ADMIT

Dear God,

I admit that I need you. I cannot reach you by myself. I admit that I fall short of your standards. I admit I have sinned. And I know that nothing I can do will ever qualify me to live in your holy presence. I need you as my Savior and I need you in my life. I admit my need of you, dear God.

2. BELIEVE

I believe that Jesus is my way to you. He's the only way. Jesus, thank you for dying on the cross for me. Thank you for paying the price for my sins. Thank you for paying that price in full. Thank you for rising from the dead to give me new life and salvation. I don't get how it all works, but I am telling you as best as I can that I am believing in Jesus as my Savior.

3. CHOOSE

So, right now I choose to trust in Jesus as my only hope. I choose to receive him as my Savior. I'm making it official, God. I'm declaring my faith in Jesus, and I am asking you to save me, right now, because of him.

In Jesus' Name,
Amen.

IF YOU PRAYED THAT PRAYER, God heard you.

If God promised to save everybody who comes to him by believing in Jesus, and if you just believed in Jesus, then what does that tell you?

It tells you that you are saved.

How do you know?

Because God promised and the Bible says so. That's enough for God, and it should be enough for you! No bolts of lightning needed. No glowing lights. No emotions necessary (though they are certainly welcome). Just simple faith and taking your Heavenly Father at his Word.

For God so loved the world that He gave His only begotten Son, that whoever believes in Him should not perish but have everlasting life. (John 3:16)

Welcome to God's family!

Welcome to the mansion of God's eternal life. Welcome to total forgiveness, and hope, and freedom, and power, and peace.

Welcome to everlasting life with God, in heaven, forever.

There's a treasure waiting for you. Let's see how to unwrap it. Let's see what's next.

WHAT'S NEXT?

You have just crossed the threshold into the amazing mansion of salvation. Now it is time to explore the treasures that wait for you.

You should know that God has a plan for your life. It is not chaotic, and it is not random. The Bible spells it out in beautiful detail.

Let's use the analogy of a journey. We are going on a journey with God to heaven. Along the way, we will pass four milestones. Here they are:

1. GOD SAVES YOU (LIVE!)

Once you pass this milestone, you are secure forever in your relationship with God. You became God's child. In that instant a whole lot of very important things happened to you. God finds you dead in sin and says LIVE!! And you come alive. Our icon for this is a red triangle with the rising sun inside it, to illustrate the dawn of new life in our hearts.

But God's plan doesn't stop with God saving you. Immediately something absolutely fantastic happens along with salvation.

2. GOD BLESSES YOU (OBTAIN!)

In the first nano-second of your salvation, God made you the richest person you know. No, not in money, but in things that money can't buy. The Bible says God has "blessed us with *every* spiritual blessing" (Ephesians 1:2). We'll use a blue circle with God's hand reaching down to fill your hand as our icon.

Nothing is missing. You have a mountain of beautifully wrapped gifts waiting for you.

One way of looking at it is to say that from now on, your whole life as a Christian is about unwrapping and enjoying the things God has given you on the day you were saved.

> Now we have received, not the spirit of the world, but the Spirit who is from God, that we might know the things that have been freely given to us by God. (1 Corinthians 2:12)

In the next book in this series, you will begin to unwrap those presents.

Before you do anything for God, it's important to get clear on what he has done for you because of Jesus and his great love.

3. GOD GROWS YOU (MATURE!)

This is the longest part of our journey. In one sense, we never get past this milestone. There are always deeper dimensions of God's love and grace to discover. Always more about Jesus to learn. Always more of his precious Word to deliver us from the devil's lies. The *Grace Pathway* series of resources has some core materials when you are ready to get growing! We symbolize this with a green circle and two arrows. In the first arrow, grace and blessing flow down to you. In the second arrow, they flow through you and back up to God. God wants you to mature your new-found faith!

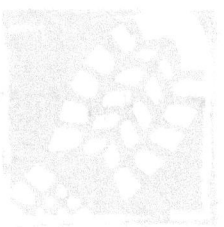

4. GOD USES YOU (ACTIVATE!)

It's the most natural thing in the world to want to spread God's love and grace — especially his gospel of salvation — to everybody you know. The Grace Pathway will help you serve God in ways that match your personality and will make the greatest impact on a lost and confused world. Our symbol for this is a yellow square with a bootprint inside.

So, there it is. The Grace Pathway. That's what's next for a person who receives Jesus.

There is one more thing, however, and it's pretty awesome. It's also a bit intimidating. Let's finish with that.

WHAT ABOUT BAPTISM?

When Margi and I were married, we slipped rings onto each other's fingers. Those circles of gold symbolize our love, our relationship, and our union. They also tell the world we belong to someone else.

The Bible shows us a way to symbolize our salvation and to tell the world we belong to God.

That way is called BAPTISM.

In the Bible, people were baptized after they were saved. This baptism has ancient roots in the Old Testament (the first part of our Bible, before Jesus was born). It symbolizes both our cleansing from sin, and our oneness with Jesus.

Baptism, as a ritual, doesn't save you. You are saved by Jesus, who died for you, through faith.

But baptism is a way of "going public" with the wonderful news that you are saved. Like a wedding ring, baptism symbolizes something beyond itself: your salvation through Jesus. It's not the ring that makes you married, and it's not the baptism that makes you a Christian. Baptism is the outward symbol of an inward reality: you are saved!

Baptism is also a mini-replay of what happened in the moment of your salvation. Just as you were made one with Jesus, so you are made one (dunked, immersed) into the water. Christ's death counts for you — so you are laid back into the water and buried underneath it. Christ's resurrection counts for you, so you are lifted up from the water and removed from it. See the illustration there? The old you is dead and buried, and the new you is alive and well.

This is how the Bible puts it:

> For we died and were buried with Christ by baptism. And just as Christ was raised from the dead by the glorious power of the Father, now we also may live new lives. Since we have been united with him in his death, we will also be raised as he was. (Romans 6:4, 5, NLT)

Your family and friends and church will see a beautiful display of your new life in Christ.

HOW TO GET BAPTIZED

Bible baptisms involved dunking a person all the way under water. Different churches do it different ways, and this is not the time for that discussion.

But the simplest way to get baptized is to ask one of the leaders or pastors of your church. They'll take it from there.

Most churches will ask you to tell a little bit about how you and when you were saved. Most will also ask you to take a class, to make sure you understand what's going on. They'll show you from Scripture why it's great to be baptized and how they do it.

Then, the big day will come, you will stand up and declare your faith in Jesus, somebody will shove you under water in a lake, or river, or ocean, or pool, or special baptism tank, and your new spiritual family will cheer the happy occasion.

It will be stressful and fun, all at once. People will be watching, so it's easy to be nervous. I get that. Unless you're an extrovert, it's a scary thing. Just go ahead and take the plunge anyway!

It will be an awesome testimony that you stand in a long line of people who have been saved by the matchless grace of God.

And it will be a declaration to God, the devil, the demons, and everybody who's there that you belong to God and he belongs to you forever!

THANKS FOR READING THIS BOOKLET

Welcome to God's family, and congratulations on finishing Milestone One of the Grace Pathway! Now that you have Jesus, it's time to discover just how secure your salvation is.

My prayer is that you will continue along the Grace Pathway, and head right away into Milestone Two!

Booklets in this Series
God Saves You

- 1 - Welcome to God's Family

God Blesses you

- 2.1 - Secure Forever
- 2.2 - Identity in Christ
- 2.3 - Growing Spiritually

God Grows You

- 3.1 - Knowing God
- 3.2 - The Cross
- 3.3 - The Basics

God Uses You

- 4.1 - Understanding Your Spiritual Gifts
- 4.2 - How To Share Your Faith
- 4.3 - Know Why You Believe (Apologetics)

For more information, bulk orders, or customized copies for your church or ministry, please visit www.MaxGrace.com.

www.ingramcontent.com/pod-product-compliance
Lightning Source LLC
Chambersburg PA
CBHW052210110526
44591CB00012B/2158